Celebrations!

Easter

Anita Ganeri

Heinemann
LIBRARY

H www.heinemann.co.uk/library
Visit our website to find out more information about Heinemann Library books.

To order:
☎ Phone 44 (0) 1865 888066
🖹 Send a fax to 44 (0) 1865 314091
💻 Visit the Heinemann Bookshop at www.heinemann.co.uk/library to browse our catalogue and order online.

First published in Great Britain by Heinemann Library,
Halley Court, Jordan Hill, Oxford OX2 8EJ
a division of Reed Educational and Professional Publishing Ltd.
Heinemann is a registered trademark of Reed Educational & Professional Publishing Ltd.

OXFORD MELBOURNE AUCKLAND
JOHANNESBURG BLANTYRE GABORONE
IBADAN PORTSMOUTH (NH) USA CHICAGO

Designed by Celia Floyd
Originated by Ambassador Litho Ltd
Printed by Wing King Tong in Hong Kong

ISBN 0 431 13791 9 (hardback)
05 04 03 02 01
10 9 8 7 6 5 4 3 2 1

British Library Cataloguing in Publication Data

Ganeri, Anita
 Easter. – (Celebrations)
 1. Easter – Juvenile literature
 I. Title
 394.2'667

Acknowledgements
The Publishers would like to thank the following for permission to reproduce photographs:
Andes Press Agency: Carlos Reyes-Manzo p14; Corbis: p8, Roger Hosking (Frank Lane Picture Library) p5, AFP p7, David Lees p9, Arte & Immagini p10, Reuters New Media Link pp11, 15, Michael S Yamashita p16, Jules T Allen p17; E & E Picture Library: Eric Marsh p13; Eye Ubiquitous: Skjold p18; Popperfoto: p12, Larry Downing p21; Sonia Halliday & Laura Lushington: pp4, 6; Sonia Halliday Photographs: p20; Trip: H Rogers p19

Cover photograph reproduced with permission of Andes Press Agency: Carlos Reyes Manzo

Our thanks to the Bradford Interfaith Education Centre for their comments in the preparation of this book.

Every effort has been made to contact copyright holders of any material reproduced in this book. Any omissions will be rectified in subsequent printings if notice is given to the Publisher.

Contents

Words printed in **bold letters like these** are explained in the glossary.

Easter time

In March or April every year, **Christians** celebrate Easter. This is the most important festival in the Christian year. It is the time when Christians remember how **Jesus** died and how he came back to life again. Christians believe that Jesus is the Son of God. He came to Earth to teach people that God loved them and to save them from their **sins**. The Easter story is sad because of Jesus' death but it has a very happy ending!

The holy land where Jesus lived.

Spring lambs and daffodils.

In Britain, Easter is in spring time. The first flowers burst into bloom and many baby animals are born. It is a joyful time of new life. Long before Jesus was born, some people **worshipped** a goddess of spring, called Eostre. This may be how Easter got its name.

Easter dates

Easter falls on different days each year. This is because it follows a calendar that is based on the Moon. Most months in our everyday calendar have 30 or 31 days. A Moon month is about 27 days. This gives a shorter year. So, each year, the Moon calendar falls out of step with the everyday calendar.

The Easter story

Jesus lived about 2000 years ago in a country called **Judea**. Jesus travelled around Judea, teaching people the way God wanted them to live. A group of friends went with him. They were called his **disciples**.

Jesus and his disciples.

When he was about 33 years old, Jesus went to **Jerusalem** for the **Jewish** festival of **Passover**. A large crowd of people came to hear him talk. Some religious leaders did not like what he taught. They wanted to get rid of him. Jesus shared a meal with his disciples, then he went to a garden to pray. Soldiers came and arrested him. One of the disciples, called Judas, had told the soldiers where to find Jesus.

Passover

Passover is a Jewish festival. It is also called Pesach. It celebrates how, long ago, God helped the Jews escape from slavery in Egypt. Many of the people who followed Jesus were Jews. They became the first **Christians**.

Jesus eats a last meal with his disciples.

The New Testament

When **Jesus** was alive, **Judea** was ruled by the Romans. The Roman **governor**, Pontius Pilate, ordered Jesus to be **crucified**. This was a very cruel and painful way of killing people. Jesus was nailed to a wooden cross and left to die. In the evening, his friends took his body down from the cross. They put the body in a **tomb** and rolled a large stone across the entrance.

A stained glass window showing Jesus on the cross.

Two days later, Jesus' friends went to visit the tomb. But when they got there, the stone had been moved. The tomb was empty! Jesus had come back to life. They saw Jesus several times after this. He spoke to them and told them to go out into the world and teach others. Then he went back up to heaven.

Bible story

The story of Easter is told in the **Bible**. This is the **Christians' holy** book. You can read the story in the first four books of the New Testament. These are called the Gospels of Matthew, Mark, Luke and John. The word gospel means 'good news'. The men who wrote the Gospels told the story of Jesus' life and the things he taught.

The Church of the Holy Sepulchre in Jerusalem. It is said to stand on the site of Jesus' tomb.

Easter messages

At Easter, **Christians** remember **Jesus'** death on the cross. This is a very sad time. But they also celebrate his coming back to life again. This is very important for Christians. They call it the **Resurrection**. They believe that Jesus coming back to life proved God's love for his people. It means that death is not an end of life but a new beginning with God and Jesus in heaven.

Jesus appearing to his friends when he had risen from the dead.

The cross is a very special symbol for Christians. It reminds them of Jesus' death and his Resurrection. You can see crosses inside most Christian churches. Some churches are built in the shape of a cross.

A child kissing a cross.

An Easter garden

Jesus was buried in a garden and gardens are also a sign of spring. Try making your own Easter garden. Fill a seed tray with soil. Plant some colourful spring flowers, such as primroses or miniature daffodils. Add a large pebble for the stone that stood at the entrance of Jesus' tomb.

Lent

The 40 days before Easter are called Lent. This is a very **solemn** time for **Christians**. They remember the time **Jesus** spent in the desert thinking about how to do God's work. This is when the **Devil** tried to tempt him away from God. During Lent, Christians think about Jesus' suffering and try to live especially good lives. Many people give up something they enjoy, like eating sweets or watching TV.

A pancake race in London (see next page).

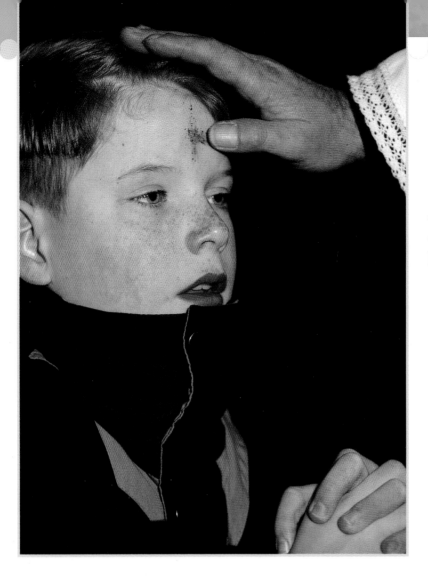

A priest drawing an ash cross on a boy's forehead.

People used to eat very plain food during Lent. On Shrove Tuesday, the day before Lent, they ate any rich foods left in the house. Some people still make pancakes from flour, milk and eggs. This is why Shrove Tuesday is also called Pancake Day. The first day of Lent is called Ash Wednesday. Many Christians go to a special service in church. The priest draws an ash mark in the shape of a cross on their foreheads. This shows that they are sorry for the things that they have done wrong. People also ask God to forgive them.

Holy Week

A Palm Sunday service.

The week before Easter is called **Holy** Week. This was the last week of **Jesus**' life on Earth. It begins on Palm Sunday when Jesus rode into **Jerusalem** on the back of a donkey. Crowds of people came to welcome him. They cheered and waved palm leaves. This is how the day gets its name. When **Christians** go to church on Palm Sunday, they are given small crosses made of palms to remind them of that day.

On Monday, Tuesday and Wednesday, Jesus taught people in Jerusalem. On Maundy Thursday, he ate a last meal with his **disciples**. This meal is called the Last Supper. Jesus took some bread and wine. He told the disciples that the bread and wine were his body and his blood. Today, Christians go to church and share bread and wine to remind them of Jesus. This is called Holy Communion, the Eucharist or Mass.

Maundy money

In Britain, the king or queen used to wash the feet of twelve poor people on Maundy Thursday. This is because Jesus washed the disciples' feet. Today, the custom has changed and the Queen gives a gift of money instead.

The Queen giving out Maundy money.

Sorrow and joy

Jesus was **crucified** on Good Friday. Good Friday means God's Friday and it is a day of sorrow and prayer. Churches are cleared of their decorations and left plain and dark. The **altar** is covered in a dark cloth, with a simple cross in the centre. There are no flowers and no church bells. In many churches, people sit quietly between midday and three o'clock, the time Jesus is thought to have died.

A solemn visit to a church on Good Friday.

A joyful Easter Sunday service in church.

On **Holy** Saturday, the churches stay quiet and dark. This is when Jesus lay in his **tomb**. But Easter Sunday is a joyful day because it is the day when Jesus came back from the dead. The bells ring out and churches are filled with flowers. **Christians** go to church to sing **hymns** and praise God.

Easter candles

In some churches, at midnight on Holy Saturday, the priest lights a large candle, decorated with a cross. It is called the Easter or **Paschal** candle. People light smaller candles from it. The candles remind them that Jesus came to Earth to light up the world just as the candles light up the church.

Easter customs

People celebrate Easter in many ways. They send Easter cards and give Easter eggs. They decorate their houses with flowers and with fluffy Easter chicks and bunnies. Many of these customs are very old. They are ways of remembering **Jesus**' death and the new life that begins in spring.

A girl with a bonnet and basket for Easter.

Many people exchange chocolate eggs at Easter. Eggs remind us of new life in spring when chicks and other baby animals are born. They also remind **Christians** of Jesus' new life when he rose from the dead. Do you eat hot-cross buns at Easter? They're spicy

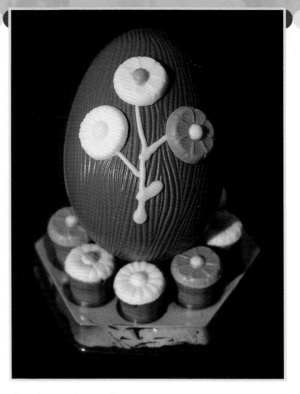

A chocolate Easter egg.

and sticky, with currants inside. Long ago, they were baked on Good Friday and given to the poor. The cross reminds people of how Jesus died.

Easter chicks

You can make your own fluffy Easter chick. Make two pom-poms with yellow wool. Make a large pom-pom for the chick's body and a small one for its head. Sew them together. Stick on a beak made of felt and yellow pipe cleaners for legs.

Around the world

Christians carrying a cross on Good Friday in Jerusalem.

At Easter, **Christians** around the world remember **Jesus**' death and **Resurrection**. But some Christians celebrate in different ways. In many parts of the world, people act out the events of **Holy** Week with plays and parades. On Good Friday in **Jerusalem**, Christians carry a wooden cross through the streets. They follow the path Jesus took on his way to the hill where he was **crucified**. In other countries, a man dressed as Jesus carries the cross. On his head, he wears a crown of thorns, as Jesus did.

On Easter Sunday, some parents hide Easter eggs in the garden for their children to find. In many countries, Easter Monday is a holiday for everyone to enjoy. A favourite custom is Easter egg-rolling. People roll hard-boiled eggs down a slope. An Easter egg-rolling competition is held every year on the lawn of the White House, in Washington DC, USA.

Easter egg-rolling at the White House.

Christian festival calendar

1 January	New Year's Day
6 January	Epiphany/Twelfth Night
7 January	Christmas Day in the Eastern Orthodox Church
14 January	New Year's Day in the Eastern Orthodox Church
2 February	Candlemas Day
February/March	Shrove Tuesday
February/March	Ash Wednesday/Lent
1 March	St David's Day
17 March	St Patrick's Day
March/April	Palm Sunday
March/April	Easter. In the Orthodox Church, Easter is a week or so later.
23 April	St George's Day
May/June	Ascension Day
May/June	Pentecost/Whit Sunday
September	Harvest Festival
1 November	All Saints' Day
2 November	All Souls' Day
30 November	St Andrew's Day
November/December	Advent Sunday
24 December	Christmas Eve
25 December	Christmas Day
26 December	Boxing Day

Glossary

altar   special table in a church

Bible   the Christians' holy book. The part of the Bible called the New Testament tells the story of Jesus' life on Earth.

Christian   person who follows the teachings of Jesus

crucified   put to death by being nailed to a cross

Devil   evil being who fights against God

disciple   one of twelve men who followed Jesus and helped him in his work of teaching and healing

governor   ruler of a country

holy   to do with God or a religious teacher

hymns   special religious songs

Jerusalem   city where Jesus died. It is holy for Christians, Jews and Muslims.

Jesus   man who lived in Judea about 2000 years ago. Christians believe that he is the son of God. They believe that he came to Earth as God in human form.

Jewish   to do with Judaism, the religion followed by people called Jews

Judea   land where Jesus lived; now Israel/Palestine

Paschal   another word for Easter

Passover   Jewish festival. It is also called Pesach.

Resurrection   Jesus' coming back to life

sins   wrong-doings

solemn   sad and serious

tomb   cave or hole in the ground where a dead body is placed

worship   to show love and respect for God

Index

Titles in the *Celebrations* series include:

Hardback   0 431 13796 X

Hardback   0 431 13790 0

Hardback   0 431 13793 5

Hardback   0 431 13791 9

Hardback   0 431 13794 3

Hardback   0 431 13795 1

Hardback   0 431 13792 7

Find out about the other titles in this series on our website www.heinemann.co.uk/library